Snowmobiling

By Laura Purdie Salas

CAPSTONE
HIGH-INTEREST
BOOKS

an imprint of Capstone Press
Mankato, Minnesota

Capstone High-Interest Books are published by Capstone Press
151 Good Counsel Drive, P.O. Box 669, Mankato, Minnesota 56002
http://www.capstone-press.com

Library of Congress Cataloging-in-Publication Data
Salas, Laura Purdie.
    Snowmobiling/By Laura Purdie Salas.
    p. cm.—(The great outdoors)
    Includes bibliographical references (p. 45) and index.
    Summary: Discusses the equipment, skills and techniques, safety issues, and more
related to snowmobiling.
    ISBN 0-7368-1058-7
    1. Snowmobiling—Juvenile literature. [1. Snowmobiling. 2. Snowmobiles.]
I. Title. II. Series.
GV856.5 .S35 2002
796.94—dc21   2001002857

Editorial Credits
Carrie Braulick, editor; Timothy Halldin, cover and interior layout designer;
    Katy Kudela, photo researcher

Photo Credits
Arctic Cat, cover (bottom left), 13 (background), 17, 25
Carl Eliason Family, 7
Comstock, Inc., 1, 21 (background)
Gary Sundermeyer/Capstone Press, cover (bottom right), 4, 8, 10, 14, 18,
    21 (foreground), 22, 27, 29 (all), 30
Jeff Henry/Roche Jaune Pictures, Inc., 36, 39, 43
Photo Network/Mark Newman, 35
Richard Hamilton Smith, cover (top right)
Visuals Unlimited/Daniel D. Lamoreux, 33, 40 (both)

**Special thanks to Christine Jourdain, director, American Council of
Snowmobile Associations for her help in preparing this book.**

1 2 3 4 5 6 07 06 05 04 03 02

Table of Contents

CHAPTER 1

Snowmobiling

Snowmobiling is a popular winter activity in North America. More than 4 million North Americans ride snowmobiles. They can ride on trails, frozen bodies of water, and in other areas.

History of Snowmobiling

In 1922, Carl Eliason began to build a snowmobile in Wisconsin. He completed his first snowmobile model in 1924. He made it out of a long, flat wooden sled called a toboggan. Eliason attached two tracks with wooden pegs called cleats to the toboggan. The cleats helped the tracks grip the snow. An engine at the front of the snowmobile turned the tracks.

Eliason attached ropes to two wooden skis in front of the sled. The rider pulled the ropes to

More than 4 million North Americans ride snowmobiles.

steer. Eliason's snowmobile traveled about
5 miles (8 kilometers) per hour.

Throughout the 1920s, Eliason built more of
these snowmobiles. He sold them to doctors,
hunters, and forest workers.

Canadian Joseph-Armand Bombardier
also built a snowmobile in the early 1920s. He
was 15 years old when he completed his first
snowmobile design in 1922. Bombardier
attached a car engine and a wooden propeller
to a sleigh. These sleds travel on four thin metal
bars called runners. The car engine powered the
propeller. The propeller then moved the sleigh.

Bombardier made other snowmobile
models during the next several years. In 1935,
he invented the sprocket wheel-track system.
Sprockets are wheels with toothlike points at
the edges. These points catch the links of a chain
or belt and cause it to turn. An engine turned
the sprockets on Bombardier's snowmobiles.
The sprockets then turned two large belts called
tracks. The tracks moved the snowmobiles across
the snow.

In 1937, Bombardier formed his own
company to produce the sleds. Bombardier's

Carl Eliason designed a snowmobile made from a toboggan in 1924.

company sold many snowmobiles in the late 1930s. Many of these snowmobiles were large enough to carry as many as 25 people.

In 1959, Bombardier and his son Germain invented the Ski-Dog. This wooden snowmobile was the first snowmobile designed for recreation.

The Bombardiers later built 25 metal Ski-Dogs based on the original wooden design. These snowmobiles were similar to Bombardier's previous snowmobiles. They had an engine

Most riders use snowmobiles for recreational purposes.

covered by a hood and a sprocket wheel-track system. But these snowmobiles seated only one or two people. The Ski-Dogs later were renamed Ski-Doos.

Modern Snowmobiling

Recreational snowmobiling soon became popular in North America. By the late 1970s, dozens of companies produced recreational snowmobiles.

Today, people continue to ride snowmobiles for both recreation and work purposes. Some people enjoy viewing winter scenery. Many people snowmobile to spend time with friends or family members. Some police officers use snowmobiles for search-and-rescue work. Some ranchers and scientists use them for transportation in rural or wilderness areas. Some people race snowmobiles in competitions.

Snowmobiling Locations

The United States and Canada have many popular snowmobiling locations. Maine, New Hampshire, New York, and Vermont are popular snowmobiling areas in the United States. Many people also snowmobile in midwestern and western states such as Michigan, Minnesota, Montana, Wisconsin, and Wyoming. Ontario and Quebec are two of the most popular snowmobiling regions in Canada.

People can ride snowmobiles on trails or in off-trail areas. North America has more than 230,000 miles (370,000 kilometers) of snowmobiling trails. People who ride in off-trail areas may ride in ditches, on frozen lakes, or in open public areas.

CHAPTER 2

Equipment

Many people call modern snowmobiles "sleds." Today, four major companies make most of the world's sleds. These companies are Arctic Cat, Polaris, Ski-Doo, and Yamaha.

All modern snowmobiles have a similar design. But some snowmobiles are designed for certain purposes. They may have powerful engines for racing. These snowmobiles can travel more than 150 miles (240 kilometers) per hour. Other snowmobiles are designed for riding in the mountains.

Chassis, Engine, and Drive System

A snowmobile is made of many parts. A strong metal frame called a chassis supports most of these parts.

Today's snowmobiles have large, powerful engines.

The engine produces power needed to move a snowmobile. Snowmobile engines use a mixture of gasoline and oil as fuel. An engine's power is measured in horsepower. Most people ride snowmobiles with engines that produce 35 to 55 horsepower. Sleds with more horsepower usually can travel faster than sleds with less horsepower.

The drive system transfers the engine's power to the tracks. This system includes the clutches, drive belt, sprockets, driveshaft, and tracks. Clutches are metal devices that turn to make the drive belt move. The clutches squeeze the drive belt to shift gears. A snowmobile switches between gears as its speed changes.

The drive belt turns the sprockets. The sprockets then turn a cylinder-shaped bar called a driveshaft. The driveshaft turns the tracks.

Suspension and Exhaust Systems

The suspension system is made up of springs and wheels. It absorbs shock when snowmobilers travel over bumps.

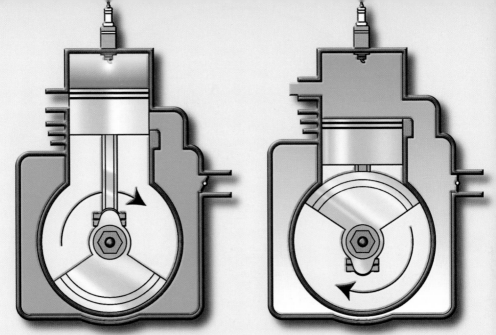

Two-Stroke Engine

Stroke 1: Compression

Intake valve opens. The gas, oil, and air mixture enters. The piston moves up and forces the mixture into a smaller space. The exhaust valve closes. The spark plug ignites the mixture.

Stroke 2: Combustion

Intake valve closes. Burning mixture of gas, oil, and air pushes the piston down. The exhaust valve opens to allow the burned gases to escape from the engine. The unburned gases travel up the backside of the cylinder and loop around. The process starts over as compression begins.

A sled's handlebars include a throttle lever and a brake lever.

Snowmobiles also have an exhaust system. This system moves waste gases called exhaust from the engine to the muffler. The muffler sends the exhaust into the air. It also reduces the volume of the engine's noise.

Handlebars

Snowmobilers use controls on the handlebars to operate a sled. They press the throttle lever to send fuel to the engine. A sled travels faster as the rider presses the throttle lever. Riders press the brake lever to slow or stop a snowmobile.

A snowmobile's steel skis turn when a rider moves the handlebars to the left or right. The snowmobile then moves in a different direction.

Each ski has a sharp piece of metal that runs down the middle called a carbide strip. This strip helps cut through snow as the snowmobile turns. Carbide strips also help sleds grip icy areas and hard-packed snow.

Parts for the Rider

Some parts of a snowmobile help keep riders safe and comfortable. Snowmobiles have padded seats. Footwells provide an area for riders to rest their feet. Footwells can help riders' feet stay in place while making turns or traveling over bumps.

Some snowmobile parts protect the rider. Tracks often pick up small objects such as rocks or twigs. Shields attach to the sides of the tracks. They help prevent objects from flying into the air and hitting the rider. The windshield directs wind away from riders. It also protects riders from flying objects.

Snowmobiles have a tether cord. This plastic cord connects to a rider's arm. The other end connects to the ignition. The cord shuts off the ignition if the rider falls off the sled. The engine then stops running. Without a tether cord, snowmobiles could continue to move without a rider.

Clothing

Riders should choose clothing that will help them stay warm and dry. They often dress in layers. This practice allows riders to add or remove clothing to keep themselves comfortable.

Many snowmobilers wear silk or synthetic fabrics such as polyester for the layer closest to their skin. Synthetic fabrics are made by people. These fabrics usually are warm and lightweight. They often absorb moisture from the skin.

Riders may wear wool clothing or a warm, soft material called fleece for the middle layer. Wool keeps riders warm even when it becomes wet.

Snowmobilers must dress properly to stay warm.

The outside clothing layer is called the shell. Some riders wear a one-piece snowmobile suit. Others wear separate jackets and pants.

Snowmobilers should wear clothing that resists water and wind for the shell layer. Many riders choose synthetic fabrics such as nylon or polypropylene. Polypropylene is a lightweight material made from plastic. Riders also may wear Gore-Tex. This breathable material has a finish that resists moisture.

Snowmobilers wear helmets to protect their heads and to stay warm.

Some jackets and snowmobile suits have flexible foam in them. The foam helps riders float if they break through ice.

Snowmobilers need other clothing items. They must have gloves or mittens. Some snowmobilers wear a neck covering or face mask.

Snowmobilers should wear proper footwear. They often choose socks made of synthetic material. Many snowmobilers wear boots with waterproof rubber bottoms. The tops of the boots usually are made of synthetic fabrics.

Helmet

Many states and provinces require riders to wear a helmet. A helmet protects a rider's head during a crash. It also helps keep a rider's head warm.

Most helmets are made of fiberglass and polycarbonate. Fiberglass is a lightweight material made of woven glass fibers. Polycarbonate is made of strong plastic.

Helmets have foam lining. This feature helps absorb shock if a rider's head hits an object.

Other Gear

Snowmobilers need other items as well. They should bring drinking water and high-energy food such as granola, peanuts, dried fruit, or beef jerky. The water and food help riders stay warm. Many riders also carry hot drinks such as coffee or hot cocoa in a thermos.

Snowmobilers must protect themselves from the sun. They should wear sunglasses or tinted goggles to protect their eyes. Sunscreen can protect snowmobilers' skin. The sun's rays can reflect off of snow and ice. These rays can burn snowmobilers' skin.

Snowmobilers should carry a first aid kit. These kits usually include aspirin, adhesive bandages, gauze pads, scissors, and tweezers. They also may have antibacterial spray or cream to protect wounds from germs.

Riders should carry a repair kit for their sleds. This kit may include a flashlight, screwdriver, pocketknife, wrench, and pliers. Some riders carry replacement parts for their sleds.

Riders should have a map of the area and a compass. These items can help riders find their location if they become lost.

Granola

Ingredients:

1 tablespoon (15 mL) butter or margarine for greasing
6 cups (1,500 mL) rolled oats
½ cup (125 mL) wheat germ
¼ cup (50 mL) bran
¼ cup (50 mL) nonfat milk
¼ cup (50 mL) honey
¼ cup (50 mL) vegetable oil

1 cup (250 mL) raisins
1 cup (250 mL) chocolate chips
½ cup (125 mL) peanuts
½ cup (125 mL) shredded coconut
¼ cup (50 mL) sunflower or sesame seeds

Equipment: Paper towel or napkin
2 baking sheets
2 large bowls
Small saucepan
Mixing spoons

1. Preheat oven to 300°F (150°C). Use a paper towel or napkin dabbed with butter or margarine to lightly grease baking sheets.

2. Combine oats, wheat germ, bran, and milk in large bowl. In small saucepan, heat honey and oil mixture over medium heat until it is thin and runny.

3. Add honey mixture to oat mixture. Mix well. Spread mixture thinly and evenly on baking sheets.

4. Bake about 15 minutes or until lightly browned. Set aside to cool for about 10 minutes.

5. Spoon baked granola into large bowl. Add raisins, chocolate chips, peanuts, coconut, and seeds. Store in plastic bags.

Makes about 4 quarts   *Children should have adult supervision.*

CHAPTER 3

Skills and Techniques

Riders need a variety of skills and abilities. They need to know how to safely handle their sleds. They also must know how to balance and adjust their positions.

Selecting a Route

Many snowmobilers take day trips. These riders complete their routes in one day and return home. Riders should choose their routes based on their skill level. Beginners should choose routes with level terrain. Experienced riders may choose routes with steep hills and bumpy terrain. Some experienced riders go on trips that last several days.

Snowmobilers must know how to safely handle their sleds over all types of terrain.

Snowmobilers can choose to travel on loop or linear trails. Loop trails start and finish at the same place. Linear trails begin at one place and end at another.

Riders should learn about a snowmobile route before they begin their trip. Many state and national parks have snowmobile trails. Riders may talk to park or forest workers to plan their trip. They also can contact members of snowmobile clubs. Many of these clubs build and maintain their own trails.

Some snowmobilers go on tours. An expert snowmobiler usually guides other riders on these trips. Guided tours may last from a few hours to more than a week. Snowmobilers on tours often spend nights at lodges or motels along the route.

Basic Riding Positions

Snowmobilers use four basic riding positions. The seated position is the most common and safest position. It allows riders to easily steer their sleds. Snowmobilers should position their body weight toward the sled's back as they sit.

Snowmobilers may kneel as they travel up hills.

They should place their feet in the footwells
and firmly grip the handlebars.

Riders sometimes kneel as they travel uphill.
This position puts their weight at the front of the
sled. The position can help the sled travel up
the hill. Riders should kneel only at low speeds.
A kneeling position often is not as stable as a
seated position.

Snowmobilers may stand to get a clear view of what is ahead of them. These riders should slightly bend their knees and drive slowly.

Snowmobilers often crouch when they travel over bumpy terrain. They bend their knees and keep their bodies just above the seat in this position. A crouched position helps snowmobilers absorb the shock caused by traveling over large bumps.

Basic Techniques

Snowmobilers vary their riding styles based on the terrain and sled movement. They should lean forward and maintain their speed while traveling uphill. They also should press the throttle lever to send more fuel to the engine.

Snowmobilers should sit as they travel downhill. They should travel at a low speed. Snowmobilers who travel downhill at high speeds may lose control of their sleds.

Riders sometimes travel sideways across a hill. They should kneel and lean in an uphill direction. This position helps prevent the sleds from tipping over.

Snowmobilers lean to help their sleds turn smoothly.

Riders lean as they turn their sleds. They should lean in the same direction in which they are turning. Their body weight helps the snowmobiles turn.

Meeting Other Riders

Snowmobilers often meet other riders on trails. These riders should follow certain guidelines.

Riders sometimes travel toward each other on a trail. These snowmobilers should pass each other slowly and move to the far right side of the trail.

Riders who want to pass should make sure no other snowmobiles are coming toward them. They should wait for a flat trail area before passing. Riders should not pass others while traveling uphill. They may not see other riders coming toward them on the hill's other side.

Some trails are not wide enough for two snowmobiles to travel side by side. Riders who see another snowmobile passing them may need to stop.

Crossing Roads and Hand Signals

Riders always should stop and look both ways before they cross roads. People in cars have the right of way over snowmobilers. For example, snowmobilers must stop if they come to an intersection where cars are crossing their path. Regulations do not require car drivers to stop for snowmobilers.

Snowmobilers should use hand signals to communicate when traveling in a group. Riders use signals to tell others when they plan to stop, slow down, or turn.

Hand Signals

Stop

Raise right or left arm fully upright; keep palm flat.

Left Turn

Fully extend left arm to side.

Right Turn

Extend left arm to side, bend forearm up at elbow; keep palm flat.

Slowing Down

Fully extend left arm, slowly move arm downward. Repeat motion as needed.

Conservation

Responsible snowmobilers respect the environment. They leave their snowmobiling area as they found it. They avoid riding over plants and control their speed in areas where large numbers of wildlife live.

Permits and Off-Trail Riding

Snowmobilers sometimes need permits to ride on busy trails. Permits help limit the number of people on the trails. Agencies use some of the money they receive from permits to construct new trails and maintain existing trails.

Off-trail snowmobilers must make sure they are allowed in places where they plan to ride. Off-trail riding is illegal in some areas. For example, snowmobilers can ride in the ditches that run along county and state highways in

Agencies work to keep trails well maintained.

Minnesota. But riding on streets, sidewalks, parking lots, and along other roads is illegal. Off-trail riders always should ask permission from landowners to ride on private property.

Sound and Exhaust Improvements

Snowmobiles of the 1960s and 1970s were noisy. The sound from the engines was as loud as 102 decibels from 50 feet (15 meters) away. A decibel is the measurement of a sound's volume. A lawn mower produces about 95 decibels. Many people believed that loud snowmobiles disturbed wildlife.

Earlier snowmobiles also released a great deal of emissions into the air through the vehicle's exhaust. Many scientists believe these substances harm the environment.

Today, manufacturers have reduced the noise of snowmobiles. They developed a device called an air silencer to reduce an engine's noise as it takes in air. Manufacturers also lined the hood with foam and wrapped the exhaust pipes to make snowmobiles operate quieter.

Manufacturers have recently made changes to reduce snowmobile emissions.

Today, the Snowmobile Safety and Certification Committee (SSCC) does not allow snowmobiles at full throttle to be louder than 78 decibels from 50 feet away. This committee works to improve snowmobiling safety in the United States. Manufacturers must follow rules set by the SSCC.

Snowmobile manufacturers also have reduced exhaust emissions since the 1970s.

They made changes to make the exhaust cleaner. They made sleds that use fuel with additional oxygen. Oxygenated fuel reduces the amount of emissions released into the air. Manufacturers also began to use movable exhaust valves. These devices reduce the amount of exhaust.

Protecting the Environment
Riders can follow certain practices to protect the environment. They should stay on trails that are completely covered with snow. Snowmobilers who ride on trails with little snow cover may damage the terrain.

Snowmobilers should be responsible as they handle trash that they create. Some trails provide trash cans for papers, wrappers, and other waste. But snowmobilers should be prepared to take their own trash home by carrying plastic bags. Some riders pick up trash left by others on trails.

Riders should stay on trails that are completely covered with snow.

CHAPTER 5

Safety

Thousands of snowmobiling accidents occur each year in North America. Riders must follow safety guidelines to avoid accidents.

Riders need to be careful in off-trail areas. These areas may have obstacles such as rocks, tree stumps, and fences. Maintained trails usually are cleared of obstacles.

Regulations

State and provincial government agencies set snowmobiling regulations. These rules help keep snowmobiling safe for riders.

Most state and provincial agencies require snowmobilers to have a driver's license or an operator's permit. People in most states and provinces need to be at least 16 years old to receive a driver's license. But people who are younger than 16 can attend a snowmobile

Maintained trails usually have few obstacles.

safety course and then receive an operator's permit. Snowmobile safety courses teach people how to safely operate their sleds. Both snowmobile organizations and state and provincial agencies may offer these courses.

State and provincial government agencies also set speed limits. Riders who travel beyond the speed limit risk losing control of their sleds. They also may receive a ticket.

Controlling Speed

Snowmobilers must control their speed. They should be especially careful at night and during snowy, foggy, or rainy weather. Riders often cannot see as far during these times as they can during daylight hours or in clear conditions.

Speed affects how quickly a snowmobile can stop. A rider who is traveling 50 miles (80 kilometers) per hour can travel more than

Snowmobilers may need to adjust their speed according to the weather or trail conditions.

320 feet (98 meters) before stopping. A rider who sees an obstacle too late may crash into it.

When stopping, snowmobilers should lightly press the brake lever. Riders who press the brake lever too hard can cause the track to stop moving. A sled with a locked track can easily skid out of control.

Frostbite Stages

Frostbite most commonly affects the fingers, toes, ears, cheeks, and nose. It is most likely to affect uncovered body parts. The seriousness of frostbite can depend on the outside temperature, wind speed, and dampness of the skin. It also can vary according to the length of time the area of skin was exposed to cold conditions. Frostbite has three stages:

Stage 1

Frostbite in stage one sometimes is called frostnip. Numb, soft skin is a symptom of frostnip. Affected skin often turns white. People can recover from this stage quickly by breathing on the skin or soaking the skin in warm water for about 15 minutes. People also may tuck frostnipped fingers inside their clothing next to warm skin. The frostnipped area may appear red after it warms.

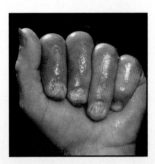

Stage 2

Frostbite in stage two sometimes is called superficial frostbite. It causes skin cells to freeze and form ice crystals. The ice crystals may cause the blood vessels to clot or clump. The skin often forms blisters as it warms. These sore bubbles of skin are filled with liquid. The skin often is white and numb. It may look waxy. The frozen outside layer of skin can cause the skin to feel slightly stiff. But the inside skin layer usually is unaffected. Only trained medical workers should treat frostbite at this stage.

Stage 3

Frostbite in this stage is sometimes called deep frostbite. The skin may be white, white-gray, or gray-blue. The skin feels hard because both the inside and outside skin layers are frozen. Frostbite in this stage may freeze muscles, nerves, and bone. Only trained medical workers should treat frostbite at this stage.

Riders should travel slowly on ice. A snowmobile's brakes cannot stop the sled on ice as quickly as they can on snow.

Hypothermia and Frostbite

Snowmobilers face cold weather dangers. Riders who become too cold may get hypothermia. This condition occurs when a person's body temperature becomes too low. Signs of hypothermia include shivering, slurred speech, and confusion. It may cause death. Some riders who fall through the ice die of hypothermia or drown. The water causes people to become cold quickly.

Cold temperatures also can cause frostbite. This condition occurs when the skin freezes. Frostbitten skin often becomes white and waxy. Frostbite can cause permanent injuries to the skin.

Weak Ice

Weak ice is a danger for snowmobilers. Many snowmobilers ride on frozen bodies of water. But riders can fall through weak ice. Ice should be at least 8 inches (20 centimeters) thick to hold a snowmobile's weight.

Riders should check the ice thickness before they ride on frozen water. Local newscasts and newspapers may report the area's ice thickness.

Riders should stay at least 5 feet (1.5 meters) away from areas of open water. They should never try to jump a sled over an open water area.

Other Guidelines

Snowmobilers should follow other safety guidelines. They should ride with at least one other person. Partners can help if a rider becomes injured. They also can help if a sled breaks down. Snowmobilers should leave a written plan with someone at home before their trip. This plan should include their expected snowmobiling location and return time.

Partners can help one another if a sled breaks down or becomes stuck in snow.

Safe snowmobilers set a good example for others. They follow regulations and safety guidelines. They know what to do if an emergency occurs. These snowmobilers know that staying safe is the best way to have fun.

Words to Know

chassis (CHASS-ee)—the frame on which the body of a snowmobile is built

clutch (KLUHCH)—the metal device that connects and disconnects a drive belt; clutches shift gears.

emissions (i-MISH-uhns)—substances released into the air by a snowmobile's engine

hypothermia (hye-puh-THUR-mee-uh)—a condition that occurs when a person's body temperature becomes too low

propeller (pruh-PEL-ur)—a set of rotating blades that provides force to make an object move

sprocket (SPROK-it)—a wheel with a rim made of toothlike points that fit into the links of a chain or belt

throttle (THROT-uhl)—a grip or lever that controls how much fuel and air flow into an engine

44

To Learn More

Dubois, Muriel L. *Snowmobiles.* Wild Rides! Mankato, Minn.: Capstone High-Interest Books, 2002.

Mara, William P. *Snowmobile Racing.* MotorSports. Mankato, Minn.: Capstone Books, 1999.

Payan, Gregory. *Essential Snowmobiling for Teens.* Outdoor Life. New York: Children's Press, 2000.

Useful Addresses

American Council of Snowmobile Associations
271 Woodland Pass
Suite 216
East Lansing, MI 48823

Canadian Council of Snowmobile Organizations
P.O. Box 1000
Station "M"
Montreal, QC H1V 3R2
Canada

International Snowmobile Manufacturers Association
1640 Haslett Road
Suite 170
Haslett, MI 48840

Vintage Snowmobile Club of America
P.O. Box 392
Fultonville, NY 12072

Internet Sites

American Council of Snowmobile Associations

http://www.snowmobileacsa.org

Canadian Council of Snowmobile Organizations

http://www.ccso-ccom.ca

International Snowmobile Hall of Fame

http://www.snowmobilehalloffame.com

International Snowmobile Manufacturers Association

http://www.snowmobile.org

Index

THE ULTIMATE GUIDE
TO
GETTING INTO
NURSING SCHOOL